What Others Are Saying

"What I appreciate about Marc Pitman is his ability to connect the dots. I've always believed we could learn a lot from our for-profit cousins, that some creative borrowing from the marketplace could serve us well. Marc excels at taking widely acknowledged ideas from the marketplace (Seth Godin's customer evangelist opus springs to mind), and – with a bit of tweaking – making the concepts applicable to not-for-profit. Not just saying they're applicable, but showing how, turning broad models into concrete, bite-size action steps."

– Joel Preston
Vice President, Major Gifts
March of Dimes, Berkeley, CA

"This is great stuff. Your blog is my homepage and I read it several times every day. Please keep up the good work. We need you!"

– Jason W. Miller
Jamestown College, Jamestown, ND

"Thanks for your e-newsletters. You're doing a great job keeping us all on track."

– Melissa Lane
Director of Development
Sarasota Opera, Sarasota, FL

"Hey, Marc, your blogs are simply awesome. It gives me the confidence that fundraising is well within our hands!!"

– Srivyal Vuyyuri
Sphoorti Foundation, Hyderabad, India

W9-BWN-217

"Marc, really appreciated your presentation. I've been at this for 29 years and can spot someone like you who is both versatile and entrepreneurial!"

– Preston Hadley, CFRE, President
Dominion Campaign Counsel, New Hope, VA

"Your enewsletter and blog are excellent. Actually more than your content, it's your style and approach...Humor, personable, practical, authentic. You model what you preach. Feel like I know you, or will..."

– Mitch Teplitsky
Producer/director SOY ANDINA
New York, NY

"Marc, I am the president of an Association of Fundraising Professionals Chapter in West Texas ... I really enjoy your coaching. It is very inspiring."

– Wade Kelley, CEO
Midland-Odessa Symphony & Chorale, Midland, TX

"I've been receiving your e-zines for about a year now and they're great."

– Shannon Sayer
Leadership Gifts
Harvard Law School Alumni Center, Cambridge, MA

"R.E.A.L. has helped me tremendously! I think the title sounds great and the simple guide provides concrete steps to follow. I have enjoyed and benefited from your support!"

– Irene McGee
Helping Hands Home Care, Inc., Ordway, CO

"When I came across your web site and e-zine I signed up since fundraising is a topic I hear about a lot these days and do not know much about. I must say that your e-course has been very useful since it gives tips that can be used on a day-to-day basis in a not-for-profit environment even when fundraising is not always the goal of my e-mail communications."

– Annie S. Wesley Ph.D.
The Micronutrient Initiative, Ottawa, Ontario

"Hi Marc: I really like your 'Extreme Fundraising' site and read it every day via Google Reader. Thanks for your help."

– Jennifer George
Director of Donor Relations
USC Libraries, Los Angeles, CA

"I'm fairly new to the fundraising arena, so this course was very helpful. I plan to take it to the other board members at our next meeting. I've applied the 'KISS' principle many times so related easily to this concept. Thanks for your help."

– Tina Lucas
Humane Society of Williamson County, Leander, TX

Your e-class on 'Fundraising 101' was excellent! I do not have experience in the development field and wanted some basic background in fundraising. You made this class fun and interesting. Also, the convenience of a taped class that I could pause and resume made a huge difference in how much information I was able to take down on notes.

– Sharon Schuler
Seminary Relations
Luther Seminary, St. Paul, MN

Ask Without Fear!

A Simple Guide to Connecting Donors
with What Matters to Them Most

marc a. pitman

published by
Tremendous Life Books

Dedication

To Emily, my best friend for the last 13 years. Without you, this wouldn't have been possible.

Acknowledgements

So many people have helped me in the long process of writing this book. Bob Grinnell is the person who got me started in fundraising and has stuck with me every step of the way. David Dunlop inspired me to always empower volunteers and help them thrive. Dear friends like Margery Whiteman, Suzy Mink, Starr Snead, and Candy Sweeney gave me support during a very critical time—and have been great friends throughout.

Jason Chatraw endured hours of transcription and walked through the process of much of the writing. Ruth Maston took that manuscript and added incredibly helpful comments that made this text much better than it might have been. Jerry Linzy offered great suggestions, too.

Charlie "Tremendous" Jones helped give this project a motivational boost at a crucial juncture.

All my clients and seminar attendees—thank you. You've proved that the ideas here can produce incredible results.

Of course, my wife Emily deserves special mention. She's inspired me, challenged me, and endured life with me—through the process of this book and through a dozen years of marriage. Thank you!

As always, any errors in this text are solely mine.

Marc A. Pitman
July 2007
Waterville, ME

Table of Contents

Introduction 11

Chapter 1: Get R.E.A.L.: Research 15

Chapter 2: Get R.E.A.L.: Engage 25

Chapter 3: Get R.E.A.L.: Ask 33

Chapter 4: Get R.E.A.L.: Love 45

Chapter 5: Seven Fundraising Myths 51

Chapter 6: Put Yourself in Their Shoes 63

Chapter 7: Tools for Knowing Your Donors 71

Chapter 8: Summary & Resources 87

Most of the people are very wonderful indeed, they almost always wish to do the right thing, and their ultimate performance, when boldly challenged and confidently led, is usually far better than we have any right to expect. Study them and treat them well, for you need them more than money.

— Harold J. Seymour

Introduction

You're in the non-profit world because you believe in the incredible mission of your organization. So, raising money to support that mission should be the most exciting thing in the world, shouldn't it? In my years of working in fundraising with clients around the country, I've been amazed that it isn't. The thought of asking for money seems to scare most people. I think "asking for money" even outranks "public speaking" and "untimely death" on the list of things people are most afraid of.

What if you were able to learn some simple tools to help you face that fear and fund your cause? I'm here to help you do just that. I'm convinced that if you apply what you learn in this book, you'll even find yourself having fun!

Why another book on fundraising? I found that when people get brave enough to try to learn how to ask people for money, they usually run into loads of technical jargon like "LYBUNT" and "SYBUNT" and "donor acquisition." They end up more confused than when they started. And even more convinced that they can't ask people for money.

Think of the last book you read on fundraising. Did it start off promisingly only to get caught up in a morass of direct mail minutia (teaser on the envelope, not on the envelope), planned giving options (CRUTs, CRATs, annuities), and gift grids and ratios? Unfortunately, most of us that love fundraising seem to have an amazing ability to overcomplicate things, especially as we look at "the ask." But when it comes right down to it, asking for money is one of the most natural things in the world. It's as simple as story telling.

1. You figure out who is most likely to respond well to your story.

2. You listen to their story.
3. You show them points of intersection with your story.
4. You ask if they would consider investing in one of those points of intersection.
5. You thank them either way and repeat the process with the next person.

I think fundraising is one of the most exciting adventures in the world! In fundraising, your equipment is often simply a cup of coffee and your passion; your uniform a suit (and a bow tie for the really extreme); your playing field a table at the local Starbucks. I like to call fundraising an "extreme sport"—all the adrenaline rush of bungee jumping but no risk of falling. There's nothing quite like the rush of helping people connect their finances with their passions. It's like putting a plug into a socket: electric!

That's why I wrote this book. I want to help you neutralize your fear. I want to become your coach and help you recapture the excitement that originally brought you into the nonprofit world. Professional development staff will get a lot out of this book, but I'm particularly writing to board members and volunteer solicitors. Statistically, chances are you'll be there longer than any staff member. In many ways, you're the most important person that nonprofit has. You are the future of your nonprofit. And your fundraising actions will leave a legacy for generations. Who wouldn't get excited about that?!

Throughout this book, I will show you some of the secrets to successfully asking for money in a way that will put the "fun" back into fundraising. Instead of dreading fundraising and viewing it as a necessary evil, I will show you can connect not just with potential donors' check books but also with their lives. As you discover the passions and the stories at the core of your donors, you may be surprised at what you find—and that discovery may be even greater than simply funding your nonprofit's latest and greatest project.

I'm a firm believer in keeping things simple. Simplicity has a beauty of its own. Especially in fundraising. So I've distilled the process of successful fundraising to the acronym "R.E.A.L.":

- Research
- Engage
- Ask
- Love

I often exhort participants in my training seminars to "Get R.E.A.L."! Trying to fit into the different solicitation programs out there can make you feel like a human pretzel—you can get twisted up in knots. I want to help you unwind and be yourself. I'm convinced the integrity in being yourself, linked with your passion, will be the most effective way to raise lots of money for your favorite cause.

In this book, we'll also take a fun look at some of the biggest mistakes fundraisers tend to make, a simple way to make sure your materials connect with downers, and some assessments to help you learn to communicate more effectively with donors and colleagues. These tools will even equip your organization's current donors and raving fans to attract new donors. All the stories I use are all real, but the details have been changed to I have changed the details on some stories to protect the people involved.

The process of fundraising is exciting, especially when you're equipped to do it right. So, let's start getting equipped!

One

Get R.E.A.L.: Research

Fundraising is the gentle art of teaching the joy of giving.
— Hank Rosso

Donors don't give to institutions. They invest in ideas and people in whom they believe.
— G.T. Smith

In good times and bad, we know that people give because you meet needs, not because you have needs.
— Kay Sprinkel Grace

He who allows his day to pass by without practicing generosity and enjoying life's pleasures is like a blacksmith's bellows—he breathes but does not live.
— Sanskrit Proverb

Do you enjoy asking for money? I absolutely love it! I like to think of the fundraiser as holding an electrical cord (the donor's interests) and facing a wall of outlets (various aspects of the fundraiser's organization). The fundraiser's job, whether as a volunteer like a board member or as a professional development officer, is to get to know the donor well enough to know which outlet fits the electrical cord's prongs. When the fundraiser plugs it in by asking for the gift, bang! The power starts to flow!

The first time I asked for money as a development officer was electrifying for me. My mentor had been intending to take me on solicitations but it never happened. I think it would've felt odd to go with him since he had developed such great relationships with these people. Can you imagine saying, "I know we're friends but I'm taking this new guy along so he can study how I'm asking you for money"? Seems weird, doesn't it?

So, I researched my first solicitation and went to do it. A parent of a student was involved in a fatal accident the previous year while on a business trip. So my strategy was to ask the surviving parent to ask the company that had employed his wife to consider a six-figure gift to name part of our newest building in memory of her. The project was an exciting match of the donor's family interests with the organization's strategic priorities.

I arrived at the person's house, had a wonderful time visiting, and steered the conversation toward "the ask." It felt really natural. He said he would think about it. I felt elated.

Not until I returned to my office did I realize I had asked him on the anniversary of his wife's accident. I was so embarrassed. You can imagine the awful pit in my stomach. I had done research but I hadn't done enough research! We didn't get that gift. But fortunately, we didn't lose his relationship either. In fact, in the end, he seemed far less disturbed about the whole thing than I was. I think he was impressed by my thoughtful attempt to match his family's interests with a pre-determined need on campus.

Even with that experience, I knew I was hooked. I'd been bitten by the fundraising bug. Trying to match the donor's interests—the electric cord—and the organization's pre-established strategic priorities—the outlets—was wonderful. I knew I was possibly helping this donor make a meaningful connection to something that mattered to him.

However, talking with colleagues and clients over the years, I realize that most people aren't as eager to ask for money as I am. My work with them leads me to believe that most of this fear is fear of the unknown. This is often expressed in terms of "What if…" questions: What if I offend the prospect? What if I embarrass myself? What if they ask me a question I can't answer? What if…? What if…? What if…?

Most of us aren't brought up asking for money—other than from our parents—so we think we have to become someone else when we do ask. The good news is we can be exactly who we are and still be successful fundraisers!

As I mentioned in the introduction, during my seminars and trainings I tell my audiences that they need to get "R.E.A.L." Research, Engage, Ask and Love comprise this simple four-step formula. It's designed to help you get as excited about asking for money as I am. In this chapter, we're going to investigate research.

RESEARCH

Research is the process of going up alleys to see if they are blind.
– Marston Bates

If we knew what it was we were doing, it would not be called research, would it?
– Albert Einstein

Action precedes funding
Planning precedes action.
–Unknown

Most people seem to be afraid of asking for money because they don't have a clue how the prospective donor will respond. Let me show you how research, doing our homework before we ask, helps conquer this fear.

Michael Wyland of Sumption & Wyland, a law firm in South Dakota, told me about a non-profit organization asking a multi-billion dollar company to become a corporate sponsorship of a duck race. This company was a perfect prospect. It made sense that they'd be willing to give. But the duck race coordinators only asked them for $250! The company did become a sponsor, but at a far lower level then they were capable of giving. The organizers had no idea what this corporation was worth! They hadn't done their homework. They could've asked for much more. But now, it'll be very hard to go to this company next year and ask for a gift of $25,000.

All of us make mistakes like this from time to time. It's just about inevitable—no matter how well you know your stuff. But you can reduce the frequency of these mistakes with some simple research.

Online and Outsourcing

It's important to strategize your campaign goal. One of the most powerful research tools is creating a "gift table." Gift tables help save you from "to-raise-$100,000-we-just-need-to-get-$100-from-1000-people" thinking. Decades of fundraising research show that money doesn't come that way. One of the great tools for you to use is a gift range calculator. There's a wonderful free resource that helps you create a gift table at blackbaud.com/resources/giftrange/giftcalc.aspx.

For instance, to raise $100,000, most gift tables will say you'll need to have the first gift be at least 10% of the goal, i.e. $10,000. The next three should add up to about 15%, maybe one at $7,500 and a couple at $5,000. I prefer to be more conservative. Look for the first gift to be 25-50% of the goal.

Goal Amount:	100000		Calculate		
Gift Range	**No. Gifts required**	**No. Prospects required**	**Subtotal**	**Cumulative total**	**Cumulative percentage**
$10,000.00	1	4	$10,000.00	$10,000.00	10%
$7,500.00	1	4	$7,500.00	$17,500.00	18%
$5,000.00	2	8	$10,000.00	$27,500.00	28%
$3,500.00	3	12	$10,500.00	$38,000.00	38%
$2,800.00	3	12	$8,400.00	$46,400.00	46%
$2,300.00	5	20	$11,500.00	$57,900.00	58%
$2,000.00	7	28	$14,000.00	$71,900.00	72%
$1,500.00	7	28	$10,500.00	$82,400.00	82%
$1,000.00	10	40	$10,000.00	$92,400.00	92%
Under $1,000.00	15	60	$7,600.00	$100,000.00	100%
Totals	54	216		$100,000.00	

An example of a $100,000 gift range chart from the gift range calculator from the Blackbaud website.

Take a look at the example chart. Can you see that you need 4-5 prospects with the ability to make that gift at each level? Using the example above, you'd need 4-5 prospects able to make the $10,000 gift and 8-10 to make the $500 gifts.

Fundraising expert Jerry Linzy of Jerry Panas, Linzy & Partners told me that, "Our experience demonstrates you need 3 or 4 probable donors to secure the gift. We also prefer the lead gift to be 15% to 20%, not 10%. We find today that the top 20 to 50 gifts need to represent half the goal."

This fact is worth the price of this book.

How do you find if your donors are able to make that kind of gift? As you can see, doing your homework here is incredibly important.

One of the best tools for this kind of homework is probably one you're already using it for other web related tasks: Google.com. Type the name of the person you want to approach in the Google search box and see what comes up. It's pretty amazing how much public information is out there on people.

It may be helpful to put their name in quotes and spell out the state you live in to narrow the search. What's really fun is pulling up information that is out of the ordinary. You may find a book review that a person wrote or a club that they're a part of. While those things shouldn't necessarily be mentioned during your visit, you will have a much clearer picture of the person when you meet with them.

Be careful not to rely on Google alone! If you type in my name, half the sites that come up for "Marc Pitman" are for a guy who's starred in horror movies with names like "Roadkill" and "Deadbeat at Dawn." It's a riot, but it's not me! (I wonder if anyone thinks it is me.) Please be sure to take your Google findings with a grain of salt.

Google isn't the only internet tool. For a treasure trove of similar online research tools, check out the University of Vermont's Research Tools Page (uvm.edu/~prospect/index.html).

With all the web-based tools, don't forget the good, old fashioned donor files. It's helpful to look at them on a somewhat regular basis. At some places I've worked, they had file cabinets stuffed with records going back to the 1930s. You will find some fascinating information there!

Another way to research is to send all your database information to a vendor that specializes in prospect research and modeling. Groups like Blackbaud Analytics do this all the time. They have access to large amounts of public information, and they have formulas for knowing how to quantify that information. That information can be like gold to your organization, even on a project as simple as a mailing. By using this type of service, I cut my annual fund mailings from an entire database of 14,000 records to just the 4,000 most likely to make a gift. I'm saving a bundle in production and postage!

Peer Reviews & CPI Index

One of the most effective and least expensive ways of researching prospective donors is asking other people. This is often known as a "peer review." People on the development committee or solicitation task force go over a list of names one by one. They talk about things like the prospect's interests, their likelihood to give to this project, and how much they should be asked for. This can work in groups as well as in one-on-one meetings.

I love these sessions because they can be highly informative and incredibly helpful in gathering anecdotal information as well as hard data. They also help you discover the links and relationships between prospective donors and other people in the community.

Admittedly not everyone is comfortable talking so frankly about their peers. So I developed the CPI Index. The CPI Index is a form of research that attempts to "objectify" the information. Rather than talking with each other, participants score prospective donors on three criteria:

- capacity to give,
- philanthropic nature, and
- interest in your cause or organization.

Capacity: Does the person have money they can give your organization? If not, he or she won't be good prospects—no matter how nice the person may be. (Face it, at some point, your nonprofit needs cash to pay the bills and accomplish its mission.)

Philanthropic Nature: Is the person a giver? If he or she doesn't give gifts to other charities, chances are high the person won't give gifts to yours.

Interest: Is the person interested in your cause? Bill Gates would have high scores in capacity and philanthropic nature, but without an interest in your cause,

he's not going to make a gift to your organization.
(Sorry if this comes as a shock.)

To conduct a CPI Index session, prepare a list of names like before but add the three CPI columns. Then ask people to score the prospective donors in each area on a scale of 1 (being lowest) to 5 (being highest) in each of the categories. When they're done, add up the scores. You'll want to personally visit people with scores of 12 or higher and invite them to make a gift. Ask the group of peers who would be the best "door openers" to help you get in front of those people.

Don't toss out the other names! Be sure to also look at the people that scored high C's and P's but only mediocre I's. You can't change a person's capacity—no matter how much you shop at their store. And you can't change their philanthropic nature—they either are generous or they are not. But you can do things to get them more interested in your organization. I'd recommend beginning to cultivate these people for a future gift. You'll probably find that many of them really aren't interested in your organization or even in your cause. But you will find a few that will become incredibly committed to your organization if they're cultivated well. Cultivating well is the focus of our next chapter.

TWO WARNINGS

Many of my clients get very uncomfortable with the information discovered in this step. It is pretty amazing how much information is public and available. You're not the FBI. You're simply trying to help your favorite organization be excellent stewards of their limited resources. This kind of research helps organizations significantly leverage the effectiveness of their fundraising.

Whatever you do, do not compromise your integrity. I promise you that all these forms of research are legitimate, ethical, and professional. But your integrity is worth more than any amount of funding you may raise for your organization. Listen to your conscience and only go as far as you're comfortable. If you're getting uncomfortable with what you're finding, stop. Ask yourself what's making you uncomfortable. Often, the largest barriers are our attitudes to wealth and money. Is that what's causing you to hold back?

The second warning is: don't get stuck on this step. This is just the beginning. The biggest potential danger in research is "paralysis by analysis." You can do homework until the cows come home, but nobody makes a gift until they're asked.

I don't know how many boards I've sat on when the inevitable question arises: "Have you researched that? I know we're hemorrhaging financially, losing money hand-over-fist, but before we fix that by actually asking people for a gift can we take a step back and do more research?" Research can be an easy way to chicken out of asking without looking like a coward. That kind of thinking will kill any fundraising effort. Sometimes, you just need to go for it and make the ask.

Research also helps you feel more secure about your ask before you even get in front of the donor. Research ends up helping the donor as much as it helps you. If you found out they've written editorials against your cause, you won't waste their time asking them to support it!

Now that we've established some of the advantages of research and some simple ways to do it, let's move on to our next part of getting R.E.A.L.: engage.

Two

Get R.E.A.L.: Engage

Computer dating is fine, if you're a computer.
— Rita Mae Brown

Relationships of trust depend on our willingness to look not only to our
own interests, but also the interests of others.
— Peter Farquharson

Don't judge each day by the harvest you reap but the seed you plant.
— Robert Louis Stevenson

I am amazed by how many nonprofit folks seem to think they can just jump into asking people for money. Think of asking for a gift was like getting married. We want to get married (get the gift) but we're scared to death of meeting people. So we stall as long as we can, staying inside, not going on a single date. But at some point, our organization gets into a financial crisis, and we can't avoid asking people for money. We really need to get married! So we panic and send lots of letters to as big a list of unqualified people—more "suspects" than true prospects. That's like running into the nearest bar and asking the first person we see if they'll marry us! Crazy, isn't it?

What's even crazier is that we get upset when they give us a weird look and say "No!"

Even if we do excellent research, it's still probably too soon to ask for a major gift. We need to get to know people before we ask them to make a commitment to our organization. We need to engage them in the process.

Engaging involves being genuinely interested in people, not just in their checkbook. (Or your perception of their check-book—some folks look well off but are simply "broke at a higher level.") Take them out to lunch. Visit them when traveling in their area. Send them articles you think might interest them. Take note of what interests them, and what doesn't. Do the courtesy of trying to find something in your cause that relates to their interests. There's no point in asking someone to make a substantial gift to a cause they don't care about.

As it is in dating, "engaging" within fundraising is a two-way process. I often let people know that in addition to being the chief development person for a hospital, I also am pastoring a new church in town. (I actually say, "I have a full-time job to pay for my pastoring habit!") You would be amazed at how comments like this open people up. I think they start to see me as a real person, not just someone trying to reach into their wallet.

Study after study shows that people give to winning causes,

not to needs! If at all possible, don't talk incessantly about your needs. I often think we in the nonprofit world look like Bill Murray's character in the movie "What About Bob?" whining to his psychiatrist, "I want. I want. I want. I need. I need. I need!" Donors aren't motivated by that. Let them know the cool things your organization is doing. This helps them see that their gift will be well used. Show them how their gift can have the most leverage on your organization's mission.

I recently met with a prospective funder to see if their priorities may match with one of our events. But I spent a good portion of the time practically bragging about some innovative things our hospital is doing. (We're one of the first hospitals in the entire U.S. to voluntarily disclose its clinical outcomes on the web. We're doing it right on our website so healthcare consumers can make an informed decision about whether or not they should get cared for by us. This takes guts!)

I feel the engage step is possibly even more important than researching. No one raises large amounts of money from behind a desk. As Si Seymour used to say, "You can't milk a cow with a letter." Fundraising is all about relationships. So get out there and meet your prospects!

Getting to Know You

As you get out from behind your desk, where do you begin? Start by exploring the interests of the person. A good approach to engaging your donors is to always remember why you got involved in your organization. What excites you most about your cause? These may be the exact aspects that connect with the other person.

I bet someone trying to watch me during my donor visits would get annoyed by how little time I seem to devote to asking the prospective donor for a gift. Instead, I love asking questions like:

- So what do you do when you're not eating lunch at this restaurant [or whatever activity you're both doing at the time]?
- How long have you been doing that?
- Really? How did you get started?

Bob Burg's book *Endless Referrals* is filled with great questions like this. I simply love hearing people's stories. I find people generally like telling their stories if they see you're genuinely interested.

Another way to get to know the other person is to look around the room or office. What awards and pictures are adorning the walls? What service clubs do they appear to be involved in?

Personally, I love books so I always look at bookshelves. Once I was in a home in California that had two small elegant wooden and bronze plaques on the bookshelves. They were two patents for freeze-dried coffee! This got me excited! Beyond thinking about the potential royalties or licensing income, I started thinking about all the challenges involved in earning a patent. This must have been something he committed years of his life to. We got into a fascinating conversation. (It turns out there were no royalties. Since he created this as an employee, the company owned all rights to the invention.)

Here are some other ways to engage people in the affairs of your organization that will help you when it comes time to actually ask them for money.

Getting Behind the Scenes

In his book *The Anatomy of Buzz*, Emmanuel Rosen talks about the buzz created by "behind-the-scenes" experiences. Rosen says we all love to feel like we're getting a behind-the-scenes look at something. Even if we know it's not really behind the scenes, we still feel special if it's an "insider's" tour.

I fondly remember Walt Disney World's "Keys to the

Kingdom" tour I took in 1998. For approximately five hours, we walked "back stage" and saw all the secrets of the kingdom. We knew that we weren't really seeing all the secrets but it sure felt like we were. The tour certainly exceeded my expectations. And for a person like me, that helped increase my enjoyment of the park on each subsequent visit.

This is also true for our donors. This is one of the reasons international development organizations host tours of projects in the developing world. These behind-the-scenes activities help donors buy-in even more to a cause they already like.

You don't need to be doing international work to give your donors and donor prospects an inside look. Here are a few ways to include your donor prospects in a behind-the-scenes activity:

- You could host a gathering at your construction site and have the general contractor or architect speak.
- You might hold a relaxed Q & A with your CEO.
- Consider giving a tour of something you don't usually showcase—client homes, residence facilities, or anything else.

What I love most about the behind-the-scenes aspect of engaging is that it often can be done with little or no expense. Since it's behind-the-scenes, donor prospects don't expect it to be as glitzy or as polished as a regular event would be! The unsophisticated nature of the event actually adds to its appeal.

At one institution, I gave a behind-the-scenes feel to class representatives by creating a monthly one-page/two-sided newsletter called "Rep Rap." Using a simple desktop publishing program, I developed this newsletter, photocopied them, and sent them out as self-mailers. The desktop publishing and photocopying was specifically intended to be non-flashy and create an informal feel. I wanted class reps to feel like they were getting something hot-off-the-press so they would know they were in an inner-circle. A glossy, four-color publication wouldn't have done that.

As fun as engaging is, don't get stuck in this step either. No prospect has ever made a significant gift just because you were friendly and engaging. People still need to be asked. So once you do your research and engage the prospective donor, it's time for the moment of truth: asking for money!

Three

Get R.E.A.L.: Ask

"No one has ever become poor by giving."
– Anne Frank

"When courage, genius, and generosity hold hands,
all things are possible."
– Unknown

"It is more rewarding to watch money change the world
than to watch it accumulate."
– Gloria Steinem

"The greatest use of a life is to spend it on something that
will outlast it."
– William James

"Much is required from those to whom
much is given."
– Luke 12:48

"There are two ways of spreading light: to be the candle
or the mirror that reflects it."
– Edith Wharton

I f you only could do one step of the Get R.E.A.L. process, and raising money is your goal, "ask" is the step you'd want to choose. Do you know the No. 1 reason people give money to nonprofits? They are asked.

Which do you think is easier: Walking up to a stranger and asking her to give money to your cause? Or calling a person you've gotten to know and asking them to invest in the part of your mission you know they're interested in?

Now that you've done your research and engaged the donor, asking is a breeze. The first two steps help you weed out the people that won't be interested so you can limit your asking on the people who will.

Before you start asking anyone for their gift, be sure you've made your gift. People can tell if you're committed to the cause or not. And it's so much easier to ask people to "join" you in supporting the project than it is to ask them to give money to something you're not personally investing in.

Setting up an Appointment

Sometimes clients ask me what qualifies as an "ask." For me, getting together with a donor doesn't qualify as an ask unless I've asked for a gift of a specific dollar amount. A vague, "Would you consider giving to our cause" doesn't do it. The donor has no idea what you're asking for. They may end up giving $25 and think they're doing you a favor when you'd been anticipating a gift of $25,000.

When setting up appointments, I like asking if their "calendar would allow" us to meet at such-and-such a time. "I'll be traveling in your area next week. Would your calendar allow us to get together Tuesday morning or Wednesday afternoon?" I find that wording makes the process of setting up an appointment less confrontational. Some would argue against using this phrasing saying it let's them off the hook because they're not taking personal responsibility for their time. But I'm not there to be their life coach. I'm there to raise money. Asking if "their calendar" will allow us to get together feels less confrontational to me.

I always let them know the purpose of the visit. I've gone into a few solicitations without letting people know I was going to ask them for money and I always felt scummy when I came around to asking. I felt like I pulled a "bait-and-switch." So when I'm setting up an appointment to ask for money I always make sure the donor prospect knows that I'm expecting to ask them to invest in my cause.

You might say something as simple as, "I'm going to be in the area and I would love to get together with you and talk about a big project we're working on." You could even say something as specific as, "While we're together, I'd really like to talk about your involvement in our annual campaign." Just do the courtesy of letting them know in advance. It makes your meetings so much easier. If you've developed a relationship with them this far, they know your job is to invite people to invest in your cause. They're waiting for you to make the ask. A solicitation isn't going to surprise them.

One of the oddest alumni meetings I've had was in Boston a few years ago. After tossing back a couple of martinis (him not me), the alumnus said, "Aww [expletive]! I forgot my checkbook. You never see the alumni director without your checkbook!" It was as though he had been given a script before our meeting! He knew what to say. I honestly hadn't come to ask him for money this time. But he knew that non-profits need philanthropic support and that relationships with donors are a kind of dance.

Given an invitation like that, and having listened to him talk about his buying three or four $1,500 suits each year, I asked if he'd consider giving up one suit and make a donation to the school. It didn't work but he was impressed that I was actually listening to him and asked him something related to his life.

Finding an Outlet

As I said in the introduction, I'm a firm believer in keeping things simple. Simplicity has a beauty of its own. I fear we're running the risk of making things too difficult as we look specifically at the step of asking. When it comes right down to it, asking for money is simply story telling.

1. Figure out who is most likely to respond well to your story.
2. Give those people the opportunity to tell you their story.
3. Show them points of intersection with your story.
4. Ask if they'd consider investing in one of those points.
5. Then go and tell that story to the next person.

Not all prospects give you such an open door as my experience in Boston. But solicitations can be some of the most fun experiences of your life.

Remember my analogy of the fundraiser looking for the connection between the donor's electrical cord and the non-profit's outlet? Asking is inviting them to plug into your cause. That's where the power is released! Remember the things that get them excited. If they don't care about "a hand up and not a hand out," don't talk about that aspect of your mission, even if it's normally a big part of your prepared solicitation speech. Focus on what it is that turns them on and ask them to invest in that.

Using Props

One of my major goals is to help you feel comfortable enough to consider asking people to invest in your favorite cause, especially if you're not a paid professional development officer. (I hope this book is helpful to them, too!) So let's take a look at some of the different tools that will help you in this process of asking for money.

Even with the best preparation, asking for a gift can some-times be a bit nerve-wracking. Have you ever set up a solicitation appointment and gone to the meeting only to chicken out of asking? I'm sure it's happened to all of us. We leave feeling like we've really let our organization down. Worse, the donor leaves confused because we'd set up the appointment specifically to ask them for money.

One of the best ways to help keep you from doing that is by using props. There's a wonderful power in putting a piece of paper on the desk or propping a picture on a bookcase. All of a sudden, the solicitation is no longer you against them. Instead, you're both focusing on the same thing. It's as though you've moved over to their side of the table and formed a brief partnership.

One of the easiest props to use is the gift grid you created during the research stage. (If you didn't do it then, try it now. You can create one for free by going to blackbaud.com/resources/giftrange/ giftcalc.aspx.) This is one of my favorite props. I find many people have a real problem asking for a specific dollar amount, say $25,000. With a gift grid, you can simply point to a section of the grid and ask, "Would you consider giving at this level?" The prospect still has a very specific idea of what you're asking for. There's no ambiguity. Even better, they can see the entire range of gifts. He just may say, "No, not at that level. I'd like to give at this level." It may even be higher. That has happened!

This grid can also become a great prospecting tool. Whether the person says "yes" or "no" to your solicitation, you can ask them if there is anyone they would recommend you talk to about giving at that level. They may not be able to think of anyone, but at least you've asked. If they do think of someone, you've significantly decreased your research time on that new person. With permission, you can even call the new prospect and say, "I was just talking about this campaign with Joe and he suggested I show it to you, too. I'll be in your area this week. Would your calendar allow us to meet this Thursday or next Tuesday?"

Another prop that I believe just might be the most effective is a picture of the completed project. These are often called renderings or perspectives. Get an artist to paint a picture of what the room will look like when it's finished. If this sort of project has been completed somewhere else, get the picture of what it looks like.

Not only will the picture communicate what you're intending to do, it also shows the prospect that such a project can be completed successfully. This is significant. All of us want to know we're investing a winning cause, to a project that actually will be accomplished. A picture like this can assure donors that you'll see this project through to completion.

Here's a lesson from experience: Try to tell as much of the story as possible in your images. Recently, we used floor plans to help us tell the story of our current expansion. We told donors that the expansion almost doubled our floor space. But we only had floor plans that showed what the facility would look like in the future.

These floor plans would've been far more impressive if the original footprint were somehow marked on them. Then they could see what the old space was and how this new space would be so much better. And they wouldn't have to take your word about the doubling of floor space; the evidence would be directly in front of them. People knew the building as it has been for the last 30 years. Having the original foot-print would've made it easier for them to orient themselves.

One important note: don't use the prop as a substitute for asking. A danger with great props is you'll succumb to the temptation of just popping them in the mail with a personal note. I call this the Field of Dreams Fallacy and discuss it in the Chapter 7 Fundraising Myths as Fundraising Myth #1. Don't give in to the temptation! Make sure to P.Y.I.T.S.—put yourself in their shoes. Would you make a significant gift if you received a gift grid in the mail? Probably not. So don't risk it with your prospect. Your cause is too important. Get on the phone, set up the solicitation appointment and bring the prop with you. You'll be glad you did!

Tangibilitize Your Ask

Props can be a big help in asking for money. Another help is tangibilitizing your ask. You won't find "tangibilitize" in the dictionary, but you will find it in practice all around you. Look at any piece of direct mail you receive that's trying to get you to spend money. The good ones will break down "what you'll get" for the cost of the investment. These concrete examples help make the offer tangible. In a way, tangibilitizing is all about taking someone's abstract gift of money and making it real.

Once again, put yourself in the shoes of the donor. Someone's just asked you to give $1,000 to her project. They've done a wonderful job presenting their case and you're convinced they're doing incredible work. But give $1,000 from your personal account? Where will that come from?! And how would your $1,000 really help them?

A great example of this was on the leadership giving page of the Alfond Youth Center (aplaceforkidstogo.org/leadership.html). There was a section starting with this phrase: "Your membership will enable a disadvantaged child to receive..." I love it! According to this page, my $1,000 would provide:

- A full year of After School programming.
- Hot meals daily.
- Camp scholarships.
- The child's choice of a variety of enrichment programs.

That makes my $1,000 tangible. I could supply a kid with hot meals every day! Looks like my $1,000 will do lots of great things. I can get my heart behind that.

The Heifer Project tangibilitizes extraordinarily well, too. Go to www.heifer.org and look at their gift catalog.

All sorts of gift ranges represented by different animals:
- $500 gift is symbolized as a gift of a heifer,
- $120 a gift of a pig,

- $60 a trio of rabbits,
- $20 a gift of chickens.
- $5,000 gift is "a gift of an ark"!

Every gift in the catalog describes the many ways people will be benefited. For example, chickens help Mrs. Ndagurwa scratch up and fertilize her vegetable garden and their 200+ eggs per year add protein to her family's diet and cash to help her market her vegetables. Can you see how much more compelling a "gift of chickens" can be than simply asking for $20?

What I love about Heifer.org is the clear statement right under the image of the animals:

"The prices in this catalog represent the complete livestock gift of a quality animal, technical assistance and training. Each purchase is symbolic and represents a contribution to the entire mission of Heifer International. Donations will be used where needed most to help struggling people."

image courtesy of www.heifer.org

With a statement like that, you know exactly what you're giving to and how the gift will be used.

How can you tangibilitize your favorite cause? Why not stop right now and find the answers to these questions:

- How many people will be served by a gift of $1,000?
- How many days (or hours) of programming will a gift of $5,000 fund?
- How many meals will be served? Jobs created? Students assisted?

As you make your solicitation tangible, remember to not overwhelm the other person with too many options. (Refer to Fundraising Myth #3 the "Cheez-It Treatment.") It's important to have lots of ways to tangibilitize your ask, but use only the one or two that will best fit with the other person's interests.

Watch Your Phrasing

Finally, when we're asking for money, we'd do well to take the advice of Mayor Shin in the musical "The Music Man." Mayor Shin always seems to be warning people, "Watch your phraseology!" Any of us could choose the wrong words for the wrong donor and turn ourselves red with embarrassment. (Refer to Fundraising Myth #4 "Mrs. McTat's House of Cat's.")

It's important to practice phrases we should use. I think one of the best phrases to practice is:

"I'd like to ask you to consider a gift of $25,000 to the campaign."

Stop for a minute and say it out loud. Now keep practicing until it rolls off your tongue. This phrase will be one of the most valuable tools in your fundraising tool belt. Since you've already made your own gift, you could easily change that phrase to be:

"Would you consider joining me in making a gift of $25,000 to the campaign?"

or

"Would you consider joining me in supporting the campaign with a gift of $25,000?"

Whenever people have objections to giving when you make an ask, it's always good to be prepared with an affirming response. You might respond with a phrase like, "I can appreciate that ..." and let the silence fill the air. Watch what happens. Sometimes people just need to hear themselves explain why a gift is so important. It's hard to be quiet at times like this but it's crucial.

I like to ask for the total amount up front. Then BE QUIET. Let your ask sink in. Your cause is worthy of this level of investment. It's worthy of their making it a top priority.

I've been told, "Make the ask and SHUT UP. He who speaks next...loses." I'm not sure I like the confrontational nature of the statement...but it sure is the truth!

Once they've spoken, help them figure out how it could work. For example, a gift of $1,000 is also $84/month.

Dealing with Objections

Have you ever asked for a gift and gotten neither a yes nor a no? Generally these are called "objections." I used to fear objections because I was afraid I wouldn't have the right answer. So I hoped they simply wouldn't have any objections. Over the years, I've come to see objections are good. In most cases, they are an indication from the prospect that they are interested in learning more. Objections are actually the start of the conversation.

Sales guru Zig Ziglar claims that for any given sales experience, there are generally only four or five objections. If that's true, why not pull your team together and have a brainstorm session? Put all the objections to making a gift to your cause—real, imagined, and off-the-wall—on sticky notes. Then put them up on the wall and try to clump them into similar categories: the "my kids are in college" category, the "this has been a hard year for my business" category, and so on. You'll probably find they fit into four or five areas.

Now that you know what the most common objections are, brainstorm answers. As the group starts showing how these gifts are possible, the synergy becomes infectious. Now you can have prepared phrasing for peoples' objections. These can even be worked into your "engage" activities or your "ask" presentation.

One phrase I've found to be very helpful is "I can appreciate that." No matter what they say, you're ability to appreciate it—even if you don't agree—helps them feel less defensive. Another is the "Feel, Felt, Found" technique: "I know how you feel. I felt the same way. Here's what I found..." This is particularly helpful if you did feel the same way as the prospect.

Another effective method for working with objections comes from Jeffrey Fox's book *How to be a Rainmaker*. Fox recommends turning objections into objectives. If the prospect's objection is, "I can't possibly give to the campaign with both of my kids in college." You can answer, "So our objective is to figure out how to make it so you can make the gift you want to to the campaign while spreading the pledge payments to make tuition payments easy. Is that it?" By turning the objection into an objective, you've put yourself on the same side of the table as the other person. Now you both are working together to figure out how to help the donor make the gift. You've taken a possibly challenging problem and made solving it a team effort.

So you've asked. Chances are they'll make a gift at some level. But sometimes even with all the great work you've done, they decide not to give. That brings us to the final phase of the Get R.E.A.L. process: Love.

Four
4

Get R.E.A.L.: Love

Be thankful for what you have; you'll end up having more. If you concentrate on what you don't have, you will never, ever have enough.
- Oprah Winfrey

The deepest principle in human nature is the craving to be appreciated.
- William James

Appreciation can make a day—even change a life. Your willingness to put it into words is all that is necessary.
- Margaret Cousins

Silent gratitude isn't much use to anyone.
- Gladys Browyn Stern

Feeling gratitude and not expressing it is like wrapping a gift and not giving it.
- Unknown

The meeting of two personalities is like the contact of two chemical substances: if there is any reaction, both are transformed.
- Carl Jung

Friendship is certainly the finest balm for the pangs of disappointed love.
- Jane Austen

*C*ongratulations! You've done your research; you've engaged your prospect, you've asked them for money, and you've answered their objections. So, what do you do now?

If they say, "Yes! We are thrilled to give you a gift at the level you asked for," then you're a happy camper. Send them a hand written thank you. (I prefer using blue pens. I've heard people respond better to blue. This may be because it looks more "real" than something run through a printer.) I've heard we should thank people at least seven times before we ask them to invest again. Follow that with a more formal thank you they can file with their tax information. And be sure to keep inviting them to "engagement" events.

I find it helpful to think of the Get R.E.A.L. process as a circle:

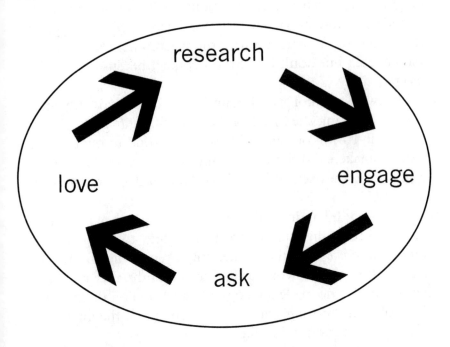

Research-Engage-Ask-Love looping back to Research.

But what if after all your hard work they still say, "No"? Do you just blow them off? Flush them from your mind? Hop in your car and yell, "Next!"?

No! No matter how badly you feel, you can't do that. Your job is to develop lifelong relationships between your organization and people outside your organization, relationships that will be beneficial to both. Walking away from someone simply because they've said "no" is not an effective way to build lifelong relationships.

People are always more important than their gifts. Stop right now and repeat it to yourself until you believe it: "People are always more important than their gifts." Besides, gracefully handling a rejection, may lead to a much larger gift later on. A "no" now is simply that…a no for now. They may make a gift in the future. If you've done the researching and engaging effectively, you had some concrete reasons to ask for the gift. Keep nurturing the relationship. This can be as simple as sending a note every few months. There may come a point where you stop interacting with the person, their interests may change, etc., but don't just cut off contact because you feel rejected.

I knew of a donor who became so disappointed with an employee leaving she asked for her $40,000 gift back. That was about 10% of our annual fund! I'm proud to say that the decision makers did the noble thing. Rather than threatening legal action, they sent it back. That kind of decision takes integrity.

They also did an incredibly brilliant thing—they convened a team of three individuals to create a strategy to bridge the donor's interest from the former employee to the entire organization. And it worked. Eighteen months after requesting her gift back, she made a pledge of half a million dollars. And she spoke very movingly at a donor event about the importance of the organization in her life.

What would have happened if the leaders had taken her to court to keep the $40,000? Or had told her there was no way in hell they would give her gift back? Even if they were able to keep the gift how much would it have cost them?

Like so much of fundraising, the "love" step is a good case of common sense. This rests on knowledge that's been around for millennia. Thousands of years ago, the revered Rabbi Hillel said, "That which is hateful to you, do not do to others." And a few centuries later, another rabbi named Jesus said, "Love others as you love yourself."

Fundraising is a relationship business. Just like in gardening, not all seeds grow at the same pace. Some need more time. Some plants grow every other year. Loving donors involves asking them when they're ready. Sometimes, loving the other person means not asking for a gift.

I went to visit someone who had been very generous to the school in the past. A few decades before, he had given a cumulative amount equaling six figures. Since then he had sort of lost touch with us. When I got to the retirement community, I asked the receptionist to call him, not noticing the hesitation in her response. She called his wife and told me she'd be right down. As I waited, I turned toward the door. There facing me was a picture of the gentleman I was going to visit with the words "In Memory Of" and the dates of his birth and today's date. It turned out he had passed away at 2 a.m.!

I didn't make any ask that day. This was one of the those sacred moments we get as fundraisers. I stayed with his widow for three hours, hearing about their life together, the trips they had recently taken, seeing her pottery kiln, listening about her kids. I was able to minister in a way few others could have. Everyone else that called or stopped by knew them as a couple. They all felt compelled to say something but not sure quite what. Most resorted to asking about funeral details. I was able to just be with her.

The last—and possibly the most important—aspect of being real in your fund raising is that of loving the donors. They have to feel you care about them just as much as you care about the organization. More than likely, you got into fundraising because you believed in what the organization was doing and you enjoy interacting with people. Don't become so focused on the gift that you forget the giver.

Even if people choose not to give, they are still valuable—they are still important. Don't forget to show them.

One way to love on your donors is to ask them how and when they'd like to be asked. Another is to find out how they'd like to be acknowledged. Many nonprofits have an annual dinner to showcase and honor their best donors. But I know of few that have asked their donors if they like to be honored publicly. Many generous people enjoy giving quietly, away from the spotlight. The most meaningful way to thank them could be by taking them out to dinner. Or involving them in a smaller reception at the executive director's house.

A Warning

Learn to create systems that make loving on your donors and prospects habitual. You're objective is to raise money. You're not around to be the entertainment director. Successful fundraising is a constant tension between effective strategic engagement and honoring, respectful people skills. You need to focus your efforts on a carefully selected group of people and you need to do that while treating all the others with respect.

I'm convinced that if we'll learn to honor people more than their money, we'll probably find our funding challenges getting smaller.

Now that you've learned the four "Get R.E.A.L." steps, let's take a look at some of the ways not to ask for money.

Five

Seven Fundraising Myths

A life spent making mistakes is not only more honorable, but more useful than a life spent doing nothing.
- George Bernard Shaw

If I had to live my life again, I'd make the same mistakes, only sooner.
- Tallulah Bankhead

An expert is a person who has made all the mistakes that can be made in a very narrow field.
- Niels Bohr

Mistakes are the portals of discovery.
- James Joyce

While one person hesitates because he feels inferior, the other is busy making mistakes and becoming superior.
- Henry C. Link

Mistakes are part of the dues one pays for a full life.
- Sophia Loren

To avoid situations in which you might make mistakes may be the biggest mistake of all.
- Peter McWilliams

I am convinced that one of the best ways to learn what to do is by learning what not to do. Now that we've seen how to ask for money well, let's take a light-hearted look at seven of the most common mistakes I see fundraisers make. I should know—I've committed most of them!

Not only are these stories instructive, they're also a lot of fun. I hope the humor will make them easier to remember and harder to repeat.

Fundraising Myth #1: The Field of Dreams Fiasco

During the board meeting of a client, we stumbled upon a perfect opportunity to make a planned giving ask of one of their constituents. The person had been actively involved with the organization for years. Her planned gift could endow an annual scholarship that was already being given in honor of her parents.

This opportunity was so good I was bursting with excitement! I enthusiastically explained how amazingly right a planned giving solicitation would be for this person. How such a gift might allow this prospect to do for the organization what she hadn't been able to do up until now. How the organization would benefit for decades to come from her generosity. And how her extended family may even get involved and give to the fund.

Then I stopped to let them discuss who would set up the visit. An uncomfortable silence filled the room. To my shock, not one of the people there wanted to make the ask. They fidgeted and shuffled their papers. After what seemed like an eternity, one person hesitatingly said, "I'm not sure we should ask her individually...What if we just sent a letter to our entire database asking them to consider a planned gift?"

One by one, everyone in the room began to breathe again. They all looked relieved, saying things like "Yeah, let's do that!" and "Great idea!" I was completely stunned; I actually called them a bunch of chickens.

They'd fallen for The Field of Dreams fiasco. In the movie Field of Dreams, the refrain is "if you build it, they will come." A nonprofit variation is: "if you send it, they will give." It seems that nonprofit boards really think people will make a large gift simply because they receive a mass produced letter.

What's the number one reason people don't give? They aren't asked. So sending a solicitation letter is better than not sending one. Most people won't open the envelope. The vast majority of those that do will look to see if their name is on it (instead of the awful "Dear Valued Person"!) and then the P.S. Very few will actually read the letter.

Here's a shocking truth: your organization is not the center of your donors' universe. They don't think about it nearly as much as you do. If the case for giving to the nonprofit were so self evident, people would already be giving more than your organization could handle.

One of the concepts I stress to my clients is P.Y.I.T.S.—Put Yourself In Their Shoes. If you were to get the planned giving letter they wanted to mail, would you be motivated to talk to an attorney to change your will?

It would probably take many letters over time from an organization you love to make you go through this discomfort. That's why in the direct mail world a 1% response rate is quite good. That means you get 1 gift for every 100 letters.

Here's a tip: If you're doing a campaign or asking a donor for a big gift, resist the urge to just send a mass one-size-fits-all letter or to say "if everyone gave just $100 we'd raise the total amount." Decades of fundraising experience shows this doesn't work. Use the steps in this book, particularly the chapters on research and engagement, to successfully reach your goal. Isn't your organization worth it?

Fundraising Myth #2: The Mickey D's Syndrome

When a dear friend of our family moved into senior housing, we had to get everything out of her house. But her new apartment was full long before the house was empty. With all the additional stuff on the lawn, it felt like we were starring on an episode of the TV show Clean Sweep.

In order to save time, I rented a dumpster. Rather than the cute little green one I envisioned, a huge construction-sized monster dumpster showed up in her yard. And it was a good thing, too! This woman was a bargain hunter and a pack rat. We threw out enough "seen on TV" gizmos and gadgets to fill up about half of the dumpster.

Only once did she get really upset—when I threw out a kitty litter bucket that actually contained an expensive compost starter. The thought struck me, if she hadn't spent so much money on "good deals" that she never used, she would have been able to buy bucket loads of compost starter.

I call this "poverty thinking." Nonprofits get stuck in this poverty thinking all the time. They become so focused on stretching their money that they lose site of quality. They will put in the cheapest cabinets in a multimillion-dollar building. Or they will bring their major donor to McDonald's to show her how frugal they are.

Most donors, especially major donors, are wise enough to know that paying a little more up front will save significant amounts of money down the road. Cheap cabinets may have saved a few bucks this year. But, due to less frequent repairs and replacements, buying a higher quality, more expensive cabinet will actually save money over time.

The same idea applies when it comes to cultivating donors. Paying a little more up front can save lots of money over time. Taking a donor out to a nice restaurant is a way of showing her that we value her, that her relationship means more to us than just the money she is giving. She needs to know that we care about her and share her interests.

Here's a tip: If a donor means enough to your organization to take her out to dinner, go to a place with real silverware. By all means, show her how well you stewarded the money she gave, but don't be a cheapskate.

Fundraising Myth #3: The Cheez-It Treatment

Have you tried to buy a box of Cheez-Its in the supermarket? I did not long ago and found the process incredibly intimidating. There are more than 10 different kinds of Cheez-Its! Some of the varieties to choose from include the following:

- Original
- Reduced Fat
- White Cheddar
- Big Cheez-Its
- Cheesy Sour Cream and Onion
- Parmesan and Garlic
- Cheddar Jack
- SpongeBob Cheez-Its
- Party Mix
- Chili Cheese
- Hot and Spicy

It took so long to look at the wall of orangish-red boxes that I almost forgot what kind I was looking for. The choice overwhelmed me enough that at first I first felt paralyzed. Then I felt stupid. How was it that I, a guy with a Master's degree, couldn't make a simple choice about a box of crackers?

Not liking to feel stupid, I left the aisle.

Oftentimes, we give our donors the Cheez-Its Treatment by overwhelming them with giving options. We think that the more options we give them, the better. Instead, we are giving them so many options that we're probably confusing them.

For example, does your web page or direct mail letter give donors the options something like this:

"You can give __$1000, __ $500, __$100, __$50, __$25, __$12.50, or __any amount."

Or does it also include a check box like this:

☐ "Please send me information on planned giving, stock transfers, creating an endowment, and corporate matching gifts."

Our intentions are good. We know there are lots of ways to support our organization, and we don't know when we'll have the donor's attention again so we want to give them as much information as possible.

But remember: P.Y.I.T.S., put yourself in their shoes. Are all these options helping motivate a donor to giving or are they paralyzing him? Options can be very helpful, but psychology experts have proven that too many options scare people away.

Here's a tip: Try limiting giving options to three or four. Rather than sending a letter to all your donors listing giving options from $10-$10,000, why not segment donors and send slightly different reply cards with only three options: something close to what they gave last year, something bigger, and something even bigger than that. In the end, the donor may surprise you and give an amount much greater than you expected.

Fundraising Myth #4: Mrs. McTat's House of Cats

FRFP #4 is all about watching what we say. In the children's book Mrs. McTats and Her Houseful of Cats, kids are mesmerized by a great story about a kind lady that teaches the alphabet while sharing her adventure of living with 26 cats. Sharing a home with 26 cats may send shivers down your spine, but it's possible that your donors may love cats. That's why we must be careful when we speak.

Stephen Nill, founder and CEO of CharityChannel.com, wonderfully illustrates this point for us in one of his tales from the campaign trail.

I was meeting with an elderly lady, 89 years old, who had

around 20 cats in her home and around her property. She was contemplating a very large gift to an organization for which I was consulting as a planned giving officer.

The conversation was going very well. Then, she asked how to go about making a planned gift. For reasons that are now lost in the fog of time, I said, "There's more than one way to skin a cat."

You don't want to know what happened next. It was ugly. Really, really ugly.

I couldn't stop laughing when I read this. How many times have we wished we could take back something we have said? You can't assume (yes, never assume) anything. Not everyone loves cats like Mrs. McTats—and not everyone loathes the animal either.

Here's a tip: Script your key questions and answers before your visit. As I mentioned earlier in the book, phrases that may seem ordinary to you may not fit the situation. Be flexible and open to using different phrases. In fact, creating this kind of script actually increases your flexibility and frees you up to enjoy the other person more.

But isn't it somewhat reassuring that none of us wins them all?

Fundraising Myth #5: The Spell-Check-Will-Catch-It

It's easy to rely only on spell check to catch your mistakes—until it doesn't catch one and you're wearing egg all over your face. Spell-check is not the same as proof-reading. Here are a couple of short stories development professionals shared with me regarding follies with spell check.

I used the word "erotic" when I meant "erratic." Luckily it wasn't in a situation where it could do any damage!

Probably the worst I can remember was in a mailing to major donors, when I learned the word public does not show up on spell check if you leave out the "l".

We've all been there, haven't we? We work on a letter. Read

it over. And over. And over. Edit it again and again. Finally we mail it. Then, when we get our own copy in the mail and see mistakes like those mentioned above!

Here's a tip: I've heard we're "spoiled" after we've read a letter we've written more than three times. After that, we need to get someone that hasn't even seen the letter to read it. If you've ever done this, isn't it embarrassing how many mistakes you've missed?

While computers are wonderful tools, they can't read your mind. Two sets of eyes are always better than one. You'll especially appreciate this when someone else catches something that you didn't see after staring at the page for hours.

Fundraising Myth #6: The You're-Good-Enough-To-Go-It-Alone Blunder

On a recent fundraising campaign, I fell prey to one of the classic blunders: letting a solicitor fly solo. (For you Princess Bride fans, this classic blunder comes immediately after "Never go in against a Sicilian when death is on the line.")

This particular solicitor was wonderfully gifted and incredibly connected in the community. She had been an active volunteer and fundraiser for our organization for decades. As the development person, I was paired up with her for the campaign solicitations. But, given her long relationships with many of these people, it felt like I might be intruding if I went on a call with her.

So when I called her to see how the calls were going and let her know I was available to go with her anytime she would like, she declined my help. She knew all the people personally and thanked me for my offer. We hung up, both feeling good about ourselves, about the campaign, and about life in general.

Then I realized the problem: we were asking people for considerably more money than anyone had ever given our organization. These asks were uncomfortable. And I let her fly into this unknown territory without me there by her side to support her. Worse yet, without accountability, it was far easier for her to chicken out.

A few days later, she dropped by my office and I was able make amends. I apologized and said I felt like I had left her all by herself. I told her I was committed to helping her make the solicitations and would clear my schedule to be with her on her calls.

She was relieved. She still needed to make the calls for appointments because she had stronger relationships with our prospective donors. But I was back in as an aide and accountability person. I was also with her at the solicitations and made sure that the ask was specific and for the predetermined dollar amount. (The Get R.E.A.L. will teach you how to predetermine a dollar amount and then successfully ask for the amount during a solicitation.)

Here's a tip: Pair up for all your asks. Doing solicitations as a pair is much more effective than going it alone. It puts everyone in the room at ease, including yourself.

Fundraising Myth #7: The Highway Fallacy

The highway fallacy comes from that ultimatum: "My way or the highway!"

In fundraising, this is when you're committed to going in there and getting that gift and entirely ignore all the clues and signals donor gives. This is a way to die a quick death when you're making an ask.

If you go to a solicitation, and the donor is clearly not interested, don't keep at it. Stop. Put down your presentation materials and let them know that you can see they're distracted. Offer to come back at a more opportune time.

Who knows? Perhaps their child is in labor with their first grandchild. Or maybe a family member took a turn for the worse the night before. What ever the case, your organization is worthy of their complete attention. And they'll be grateful for your consideration.

We'll get into this in much more detail in the next two chapters "P.Y.I.T.S." and "Know Your Donors." For now, remember that not everyone is like you. Your organization isn't the most important thing in their world.

Here's a tip: Run your ideas past a coach, colleague, or trusted friend—particularly one that sees things from a different perspective than you.

Individually, none of these faux pas will ruin your fundraising. But commit all of them and you may be lucky if you get any money!

You can avoid making major mistakes by remembering the following:

- Don't be lulled into thinking everyone understands your cause
- Don't be cheap with your major donors
- Don't overwhelm people with too many options
- Don't forget to be careful with your phrasing
- Don't fail to have someone else look over your letters
- Don't go alone on major asks
- Don't ignore the clues the donor is sending you

Six

Put Yourself in Their Shoes

Some people think only intellect counts: knowing how to solve problems, knowing how to get by, knowing how to identify an advantage and seize it. But the functions of intellect are insufficient without courage, love, friendship, compassion and empathy.
- Dean Koontz

The great gift of human beings is that we have the power of empathy.
- Meryl Streep

Friendship is a living thing that lasts only as long as it is nourished with kindness, empathy and understanding.
- Unknown

The most valuable things in life are not measured in monetary terms. The really important things are not houses and lands, stocks and bonds, automobiles and real state, but friendships, trust, confidence, empathy, mercy, love and faith.
- Bertrand Russell V. Delong

Throughout the chapters on the Get R.E.A.L. process, I repeatedly referred to "P.Y.I.T.S." Let's take a closer look at how putting ourselves in their shoes can make our fundraising far more effective.

I once had a colleague who wrote an end-of-the-year letter that drove home the importance of P.Y.I.T.S. Those of us asking people for money, volunteers and employees, need to constantly be putting ourselves into the shoes of the person receiving the solicitation. He was a numbers person who wrote the letter in a way that motivated him. The main thrust of the letter was something like:

Alumni, we need to raise more money. The parents have nearly reached their goal at 90 percent, but the alumnae have only raised 20 percent of their goal. We really need your help to pull this thing together.

She worked for weeks on crafting this letter. After a couple of us read it, we went to her office, closed the door, and told her we thought it was terrible.

As we were reading the letter, we thought about how we would feel if we didn't work with this nonprofit and we'd received this letter. We found ourselves thinking things like: "That's not my problem;" "I don't care what your goals are—sounds like you should set them lower;" and "a letter like that is not going to encourage me—or anyone else, for that matter—to give." I was very surprised by my strong adverse reaction.

Once I made a one-time gift to a large national organization that followed up each December with strong emotional appeal for money. Each year, the letter basically said, "We're not going to make our budget if you don't help us out."

The first time I saw this letter, I felt bad for the organization. Finally, after three years of receiving these letters, I called them up and said, "If you guys are that fiscally unsound and you can't manage the money you've been given, I can't even consider giving you a gift." They were shocked at my reaction. They'd been mailing this package for years. These letters actually came halfway through their fiscal year but most of their donations came in December.

If you have a sincere crisis, then by all means tell your donors! Bad things happen to the best causes. But if you're really not going to make budget and you've waited this long to communicate effectively, you probably won't be around much longer anyway. Crying "Wolf!" is a sure-fire way to get people to ignore you. As Jerry Linzy of Panas, Linzy, & Partners says, "Development isn't about meeting your needs; it's really about meeting your donor's needs."

In an effort to help our colleague, we asked him why he was so committed to the school. We knew he had wired his first annual gift from Europe the year after he graduated. We asked him why he had chosen to work at his alma mater. We asked what motivated him to ensure the school's financial future and why was he so committed to having his own kids attend the school? We encouraged him to tell his story.

This was a pretty uncomfortable conversation. But he ended up writing an amazingly moving letter, even though it was totally out of his comfort zone. And we raised more money than we had ever raised at the end of the year. You know you've written an effective appeal when people put notes in with their checks telling you that they were crying as they read the letter. People wrote to tell us how his story reminded them this school had impacted their lives and their kids' lives and how that also moved them to give.

So, before you send out a letter or make a solicitation, take a moment to put yourself in their shoes by asking yourself, "How would I feel if I didn't work in the development office and I was approached in this way?"

Take Time

Some direct mail research seems to indicate that if you don't have a return address on the envelope people will open it because they don't want to miss out on something. One organization that practices this method crafted an entire campaign around the theme "CREDIT DENIED." The idea behind it was to share the story of a family that needed financial help and couldn't get it—their credit was denied—but this organization was able to help them. Everyone in the organization was moved by this theme, the story of this family, and how well it tied in with their mission. "CREDIT DENIED" became their battle cry.

So they printed the outside of the envelopes with big red letters "Credit Denied!" Apparently no one thought about what it would be like to get such a letter in their mail box. When people went to their mailbox and found a letter with "CREDIT DENIED" stamped on it, they definitely opened it. When they found out it was a fundraising appeal, they got ticked off before they even were able to read the terrific story! When my colleague shared this with me on a CharityChannel.com listserv, there were comments from people on the list who cut the organization out of their regular donations because of that very mailing! They still remembered their shock and anger years later!

It seemed like a good idea—and it even made sense from an organizational perspective. But the tagline on the envelope scared people about their own credit so much they weren't even interested in reading an appeal.

I like to remind clients that their organization is not the center of their donor's universe. As board members and employees, much of our lives revolve around our cause. But our donors have lives of their own. Things that are self evident to us are not necessarily self-evident to them.

It's easy to get so consumed with reaching our goals and coming up with catchy ideas that we don't take the time to think about what others will see when they receive our material. Just taking a few minutes to think about the people you're trying to reach, to put yourself in their shoes, can save you from myopically doing more damage than good with your appeals.

Conversational or Scripted?

What is the number one reason why people don't give? It's simply that we don't ask.

While I'm not exactly the biggest proponent of phone-a-thons themselves, I've had to run them from time-to-time. (Personally, I don't like taking their calls, so why would I want to do it to anyone else?) If you have ever participated in a phonathon, you usually have a script when you make the calls. I've heard college graduates reading these scripts in a way that sounds like a first time reader or some bad Saturday Night Live skit. "Hi … my…name is… Marc … I'm calling on behalf of …"

Put yourself in the donor's shoes. If you're on the other end of the phone, you know if you're having a script read to you. The people trying to motivate you to give simply sound unprofessional. This is particularly bad if you represent an educational institution. Would you rather give to someone who is conversational rather than scripted? Why not help phone-a-thon participants sound like friends when you're talking with them? I like scripting out conversations, but why not have the few key points bulleted out so callers can quickly return to them?

Comfortable in Your Own Shoes

While it may behoove you to spend a good portion of your time in the planning phases of a fund raising campaign to put yourself in the shoes of others, it's also good to get comfortable in your own shoes. You have to realize the task at hand is asking people to commit money to your cause. At some point, you have to face your fear and insecurities.

If you have been involved in fund raising for 30 days or 30 years, think about the times you were afraid. Fear is your imagination going on the dark side and thinking about all the things that could go wrong. Usually, the things you were afraid of never happened any way. You could even bless someone by asking them to give and helping them allocate their resources for something that will really empower them. The positives far outweigh the negatives when it comes to giving people an opportunity to do something worthwhile with their money.

In order to get comfortable with what you are doing, you have to begin with this question: Why are you asking for money? Are you doing it to change a kid's life? To change your community? There could be a thousand reasons why you are asking for money—and why you believe in the cause that you are leading. Knowing that you are going to be contributing to something you believe in helps you gain the confidence you need to ask people invest with you. As you enter into this process you still might be afraid, but at least you know why you're doing what you're doing.

What is the worst that could happen? They could say "no." That's about it. They're not going to die on you. Often. (Refer back to the chapter on "Love" for a story of when this happened to me.)

What if the donor immediately gives you exactly what you ask for? I've heard of a fund raiser who asked for $1,000—and the donor wrote out the check and didn't even think about it. Instead of taking the check, this fund raiser was so comfortable in his own shoes. He handed it back to the man and said, "We didn't ask for enough. We don't want to be one of your throwaway charities. We want to be on your top 10 list." That spoke volumes to this businessman because he knew they weren't just glad-handing and that they were serious about what they did with his money.

Giving the check back may not be the wisest thing. But if you're comfortable enough with yourself, you may decide to apply the YMCA principle. The YMCA Principle is simply this: when you get someone to commit to giving $500, you ask them if they would be willing to give that same amount for each of the next three years. Suddenly, the $500 gift turned into a $1,500 gift and you don't have to go back to that person asking for money each year.

So as you go through the REAL process of asking for money, remember to P.Y.I.T.S.—put yourself in their shoes. If you wouldn't like receiving what you're about to give, chances are the other person won't either. So change your approach.

Seven

Tools for Knowing Your Donors

A great marriage is not when the 'perfect couple' comes together. It is when an imperfect couple learns to enjoy their differences.
- Dave Meurer, "Daze of Our Wives"

So, let us not be blind to our differences - but let us also direct attention to our common interests and to the means by which those differences can be resolved.
- John F. Kennedy

Differences of habit and language are nothing at all if our aims are identical and our hearts are open.
- J. K. Rowling, Harry Potter and the Goblet of Fire

If by saying that all men are born free and equal, you mean that they are all equally born; it is true, but true in no other sense; birth, talent, labor, virtue, and providence, are forever making differences.
- Eugene Edwards

Personality can open doors, but only character can keep them open.
- Elmer G. Letterman

If it weren't for caffeine I'd have no personality whatsoever!
- Anonymous

One of the biggest obstacles to overcome in any fundraising effort, particularly a long-term project, is that of knowing who your donors are. Sounds odd, doesn't it? You're probably already saying, "Hold on, Marc. I know exactly who my donors are, thank you very much. They're the ones that have made a gift to my project! I can print out a list of their names any time I want." I agree that is simple and important. But what can you tell me about your donors? What are they like? Old? Young? Wealthy? Middle-class? Male? Female? Professionals? Blue collar? Single? Married? Parents? Business executives? Entrepreneurs? Smart? Savvy? Skilled? Generous? Do they tend to be optimists? Pessimists? Do they like public recognition? Or do they prefer one-on-one appreciation?

Knowing as much as we can about the people we are inviting to care about our cause can go a long way in helping us achieve our goals—especially in our goals of building long-term relationships. In this chapter, I'll introduce you to two effective assessments that can help you interact in every step of the Get R.E.A.L. process: the D.I.S.C. test and The Highlands Ability Battery.

The D.I.S.C. Test

If you've never heard of the "D.I.S.C." test, you are missing out on a really simple assessment tool that will help you understand people's personality profile. The four quadrant personality assessments have been around for millennia. The labels range from the standard "sanguine," "phlegmatic," "melancholy," and "choleric" labels of the ancient Greeks to different kinds of cars. I think its popularity is so enduring because it's simple to grasp and easy to relate to yet you can spend years using it. I've even heard of one college admission office that uses this when they want to know how to address potential students. They put a D, I, S, or C in the prospective students file to help each other know how to best interact with that person. But I'm getting ahead of myself.

The D.I.S.C. assessment is basically a circle with two lines in it. The vertical line represents how fast or slow you process things. Write "faster" at the top of the circle and "slower" at the bottom. The horizontal line represents your preference of working with people or tasks. Write "tasks" on the left-hand side of the circle. Write "people" on the right. Each of these lines acts as a spectrum. Some people will be task oriented but not to the same extreme as others. In your circle with the two lines, put a "D" in the upper left-hand quadrant; an "I" in the upper right-hand; an "S" in the lower right; and a "C" in the lower left. Each quadrant has a different way of seeing the world and interacting with others.

Image courtesy of PersonalityInsights.com

I recommend you take an official assessment by a provider like that named in the resource section. But if you haven't, take a minute to ask yourself:

- Do you tend to be a faster-paced person? Someone who prefers
  to be up front and on stage?
- Or are you someone who doesn't mind being behind the scenes, out of the limelight?

- Would you rather be with people or do you prefer to accomplish tasks?

D people are up front and on stage. They're doers. They get things done, no matter what. These folks are often what people think of as the stereotypical "leader." They're the people who say, "We're doing this my way."

I people are also an up front person, but are also very people-focused. I people just love being around other people. Like a golden retriever, strangers are just friends they haven't met yet. If they have to choose between coffee with friends or working on a task alone, they're always going to choose coffee with a friend. They're high-energy people who say, "We're going to have fun!"

S people are also very much on the side of people, but they don't want to be up front. They're almost like Piglet from Winnie the Pooh, just not as timid. They're solid, dependable people. They want to make sure everyone's in harmony. They are always measuring the atmosphere, checking in to see how people are feeling. They want to know where everybody is at and how they're doing. We need S people because Ds and Is tend to be so far out in front that they're out of touch with how people are feeling and, as we'll see, Cs aren't particularly wired in a way to consider people's feelings. S people ask, "How is everyone doing?"

C people are into tasks. Really into tasks. They love numbers. They don't necessarily have a need or desire to be around people. They study and research before coming to conclusions. They just want to make sure everything is done correctly. They're the kind of people who say, "We're going to do it the right way and my way is the right way."

If you're a movie buff, then here are a few characters' personalities and how they might fit on the D.I.S.C. test:

- In "Gone with the Wind", Rhett Butler is a D, Ashley is an S.

- In the movie "Patch Adams," Robin Williams' character would be an I.
- Professor Higgins from "My Fair Lady" is a typical C.

There are many ways to categorize these personalities, but the most important thing is to understand how people communicate and process information within each category.

Shortly after starting a new job, my wife and I learned that we were pregnant. Naturally, one of my wife's first assignments for me was to find out if my employer had any "paternity leave" policy. Since I had just started there, I felt extremely uncomfortable about asking. I thought about directly asking our CFO—she who oversaw the human resources function—but I decided against it. She took things very seriously, and it seemed to me a bit negatively. I didn't want to stir anything up so I decided to send a personal just-checking-in-but-I-know-this-probably-isn't-an-option email to someone else in her office.

The very next day, instead of getting a reply from that person, I received a policy statement from the CFO herself! I was so angry (and probably quite embarrassed)! I hadn't asked her. I had intentionally chosen not to ask her because I was sure I'd get a response like the one in front of me.

There was nothing personal in the email. There was even nothing in there indicating that she knew I wasn't looking to get out of working my new job, that my query had been merely informational. There was nothing about me at all! There was just a full blown, bureaucratic, policy statement. I was beside myself! Can you tell that I'm a high I?

Fortunately, I've learned to vent in front of someone else before I blowing up in anger at the person I'm upset with. I went into my boss' office and unloaded. I took this impersonal response to mean that the CFO was questioning my integrity and thinking I was a slacker. My boss was much more reasonable than I was and helped me gain some perspective. After some time together, he recommended I talk to the CFO.

When I calmed down, I called the CFO. She had no idea she had done anything that would upset me. "I was just writing policy," she said. "Every organization needs policy to run." Of course, she was right. Every organization does need policy. If I had stepped back to see the situation in terms of D.I.S.C., I would've realized she was a high C person. As such, she was more focused on policies and procedures—the task side of life—than with relating to people. In an organization, C's know that you need some level of policies to help direct relationships within the organization. What I found out was that this organization was full of policy gaps when the CFO arrived. It needed someone who was a high C to fix them. My question simply revealed another gap, so she quickly filled it.

To a high I like me, her filling the gap felt more like she was playing a game of Whack-a-Mole and she saw me as the mole! For her part, she was amazed that anyone would get emotionally upset by a policy.

D.I.S.C. & Fundraising

Think about D.I.S.C. in terms of your fundraising. Knowing how to relate to someone will help you in being much more effective at asking them for money. If you're a high C, you'll probably tell your organization's story based on statistics, graphs, and columns of numbers. But if your prospect is a high I she would rather hear about how one person's life was impacted by your organization's work. You can pick up lots of these cues during the Engage step of the Get R.E.A.L. process.

I'm a high I and a high D. I guess that means I'm a 100% fast motor person. Seminar attendees tell me I talk very fast and usually ask me to slow down so they have a chance to catch up. I love people but, as a high D, completing tasks is also very important to me. One of the most frustrating fundraising visits for me was with a donor who spent hours touring me around her city. Hours—because that was important to her.

All I could think of was all the other donors I could have visited. At that point in my career, my goal was to pack my schedule with as many appointments as possible. I wanted lots of visits and lots of solicitations. Appointments were more about task completion than about relating to people and I wanted to complete as many as I could. That was how I could show I was making the most of my time.

Now I realize that I shouldn't be fast with someone who wasn't. As Stephen Covey says, "Slow is fast; fast is slow." I needed to slow down. This donor was investing in our relationship. She was thrilled to have a representative from my organization come and visit her and she wanted to treat me well. Taking that time with her created a relationship that produced fruit in the coming years.

This works the other way too. If you're slow with a fast-paced person, you'll probably need to speed up to keep your prospect from becoming bored. If you're working through a presentation, take the cues of the other person and move through it more quickly if you have to—even if it's faster than what you've practiced at the office. Even if it means not completing every bullet point of your presentation.

The Highlands Ability Battery

Another tool that will give you a way to approach your donors, as well as your own life, is The Highlands Ability Battery. This assessment revolutionized my own professional growth and my marriage.

In First Break All the Rules, authors Marcus Buckingham and Curt Coffman explain the difference between average managers, good managers, and great managers. The book lays to rest the common human resource myth that you need to work on your weaknesses and be a well-rounded person to succeed. Backed by all the statistical research of the Gallup Organization, Buckingham and Coffman show that excellent managers, rather than looking for weak areas, actually discover people's natural strengths and put people in positions that let those strengths flourish.

The Highlands helps you do just that. It is specifically designed to help identify your "hard-wired" natural abilities. Natural abilities are the things that come easily to you. Most often, the stress we feel in life comes from either operating in areas that do not come naturally to us or from abilities that aren't being used. As we arrange our lives more in line with our natural talents, we find stress practically evaporates and our work becomes filled with a renewed energy and purpose.

Through a three to four-hour test full of 19 seemingly mind-numbing work samples you complete within set time limits, the Highlands measures which tasks you complete quickly and which take you more time. All of us could complete all the tasks if we were given enough time. The ones that come quickly point to your hard-wiring, your natural talents.

One of the things I love most about the Highlands is that you can't skew the results. All the other personality assessments I've used ask you to rate yourself on what you perceive your behavior or attitudes to be. After you take a few, you begin to see where the questions are going and how to make the results look more as you would like. The Highlands is different. It objectively measures how well you perform on specific work samples. That's it. Either you do them in the allotted time or you don't. There's no bias to it so this method very effectively identifies your hard-wired, natural abilities.

After taking the test, you receive a very long report describing your results and how they affect your life. Then you have a two-hour, one-on-one feedback session with a coach. This coach has studied your results and is able to explain them and to see if you agree or not with them. He also helps identify patterns or "clusters" of abilities and helps you begin to strategize your life around your natural talents.

After completing the Highlands Ability Battery, my mother said, "Marc, I felt more mentally alert after spending 33 hours in labor with you than I do after taking this test! I hope it's worth it!" Fortunately, it was. After seeing the report and going over it with a knowledgeable coach, my mom was amazed. The Highlands actually helped her explain some learning styles she had noticed in herself but hadn't been able to explain. It helped her see herself in a completely new light.

And how did it revolutionize my marriage? It gave us a common language based on an objective assessment. One of the abilities measured is "idea productivity." Idea productivity measures how fast your faucet of ideas is flowing. Some people are generating new ideas all the time, others generate very few. Neither is better than the other. Some roles require coming up with lots of ideas quickly. But people with high idea productivity can't always focus; all the new ideas keep distracting them.

I'm a mid-range in idea productivity; my wife is off-the-charts! The other day, she and I were talking at the kitchen table as she was eating some store-bought pudding. All of a sudden, she stopped talking in mid-sentence and just staring at her empty plastic cup. Just staring at it. It was really weird. I thought I had lost her. And I was hoping I hadn't done something to offend her!

Then she sort of snapped out of it. "Sorry," she said. "idea productivity. I just had about a hundred ideas of what I could do with this little plastic cup." Immediately the whole situation made sense and I was able to relax. That's just how she lives her life—ideas coming in a constant flow. People who have high idea productivity have hundreds of ideas thrown against the front of their brain all the time. The ideas aren't all good but the quantity can be overwhelming.

Think about this in terms of donor relations. Do you have a donor or alumnus who is always coming up with ideas on how you can do your job better? Maybe they're simply high in idea productivity. Rather than letting them grate on you, why not invite them to the next brainstorming session your staff has? Their hard-wired ability may really help improve whatever you're talking about. And if you're asking that person for money, you know you'll need to vary your approach with props, other people, and other tools just to help them stay focused.

Let's look at some of the abilities the Highlands tests on and see how these can affect your approach to fundraising.

Introvert and Extrovert

The only subjective part of the Highlands is the portion that evaluates whether you are an introvert or an extrovert. Knowing this can help avoid many conflicts! Take conversations for an example. Introverts tend to share an idea once they've worked it over internally and arrived at their finished product. They've thought things over, they've come to a resolution, they've framed it, and they're through. Extroverts, on the other hand, start talking without knowing what the finished idea will be. They love doing the processing outside themselves and with others. As an extrovert, I practically have to speak to think. Somewhere words originate, they pop out of my mouth, and I think about them only after I hear them. Sometimes I think they're a great idea and other times I don't. So, when I'm talking to someone more introverted who's familiar with Highlands, she'll ask me, "What just went on? Did you make a decision?" Introverts tend to think things over in private and then speak the finish product.

Guess what happens when an introvert shares an idea at a gathering of people. The extrovert pounces on the idea. She starts batting it around like a cat with a ball of yarn. What she doesn't realize is the introvert hadn't offered the idea as a rough draft. From an introvert's perspective, who would be crazy enough to share an idea that hadn't been completely thought through? The idea he shared was meant to be a finished product. And now an insensitive extrovert is shredding it apart, thinking she's being helpful.

We've all been in this situation before. When teams learn this particular distinction, extroverts start asking things like,

"Is this a rough draft or a polished idea?" Introverts also get less offended when an extrovert runs with an idea because they understand that not everyone processes the same way they do.

Another difference between introverts and extroverts is what tends to stimulate them. Extroverts tend to get energy from people; introverts tend to get energy from being alone. Since people are energizing to extroverts, they prefer to be spontaneous in their interactions with people. An extrovert can be like a golden retriever, fun to have around and happy to bounce from person to person. He'll still get the "work" of the social function done, whether it's talking about the annual fund or soliciting a major gift, he'll just do it in a more "free-form" style.

Introverts can also be very social but they like to know where they fit or what their specific role is. Whether they verbalize it or not, they tend to want to know things like "Am I doing registration?" or "Am I supposed to talk to these six people?" Having specific, well defined roles for social functions helps introverts feel less drained.

This can be incredibly important when dealing with donors. For example, in one place I worked, my two superiors were more introverted. I'm off-the-chart extroverted but, unfortunately, I didn't know the full impact of these distinctions at the time. I started holding alumni cultivation events in brew pubs and other informal settings. These fit my personality so I thought they must be good for everyone. And the alumni seemed to have a blast. But my superiors found these events very draining. Now I know that I should have given them an outline of the event's purpose, participants, and their intended role. Both of them were great with people, but in a manner that's different from mine. I should have also mixed these informal events with more formal ones, like a sit down dinner. We would have more effectively served the alumni too. My guess is that the more introverted folks didn't come to the brew pubs for the same reasons my supervisors stopped going.

Generalist and Specialist

According to the research done by the Highland Company, about 75 percent of the population is composed of "generalists"; "specialists" make up the remaining 25 percent. When you ask a generalist what they do, they tend to tell you in terms of what their organization does, "Well, we help feed kids in central Africa." A specialist answering the same question will say, "I make sure that donors are cultivated appropriately and stewarded well." They describe their specific duties.

A generalist is like a casserole—all the ingredients are blended together to form an end product. Most of the specific ingredients are not distinguishable in the final product. A specialist is like a Waldorf salad. All the ingredients are separately definable—the lettuce, the walnuts, the apple slices, etc. And each of these separate elements make a distinct end product without losing their distinctiveness.

If generalists are a mile wide and an inch deep, specialists are an inch wide and a mile deep. So if you've asked the donor prospect, "What do you do?" and they answer in terms of their specific duties, you know you're probably talking to a specialist. They may not know about a lot of things, but what they know they know very well. So focus the conversation on areas that will let the specialist showcase their individualized knowledge. (Specialists love showing off what they know. That's why I've written this book!)

Knowing whether your prospect is a generalist or a specialist can also help you determine how much detail to give about your organization. Specialists will probably prefer to get to know one aspect of your organization in great detail. Generalists will tend to be inspired by a broad overview. This in turn will help you create the most effective solicitation strategy. Specialists will probably prefer to be very specific and strategic in their gifts, generalists will probably be more comfortable with fewer restrictions.

Classification and Concept Organization

Two more talents identified by the Highlands are classification and concept organization. High classification people are those who tend to love chaos and flying by the seat of their pants. They can walk into a situation and immediately spot the problems. Low classification people tend to need some more structure. They need to do some analysis before pointing out where the problems may be. People high in concept organization are able to organize everything in their head. People lower in concept organization tend to rely on planners and filing cabinets. They need lots of props to help them organize their concepts. Both classification and concept organization are crucial in asking for money.

If you're high in classification, you can almost instantly zoom in on what's important when talking with a potential donor. If you're not, then you need to form a process through which to work in order to ease in and find out what the person's hot buttons are.

The higher you are in concept organization, the easier it is for you to make things quickly understandable to others. The lower you are in concept organization, the more time it will take. You'll probably take much more time preparing your story before going into a solicitation. You may need pictures of the children in Africa or pictures of the buildings you want to construct in order to begin the process.

This knowledge can also come in handy when you are making solicitations. For example, if your prospect is high in classification, you'll need to be able to move through your presentation quickly. They will rapidly grasp the ideas you're presenting. So don't bore them, keep moving at an appropriate pace. But if you're too fast with a person lower in classification, you'll risk sounding like a con artist. That's never an effective way to ethically raise money!

What if your potential donor is low in concept organization? Whether you yourself are high or low, it will be important to have the props and pictures, even if you don't personally need them. If they're higher in concept organization, you'll probably find yourself needing to stick less rigidly to your outline.

Verbal and Tonal memory

Lastly, let's look at verbal memory and tonal memory. The Highlands defines verbal memory as the ability to take in written information. If you're low in verbal memory, reading to remember will take more time. Tonal memory is defined as your ability to take in information through what you hear. These are the only two learning channels schools focus on. The Highlands identifies three more: design memory, rhythm memory, and number memory. But let's stick with the two we are most familiar with, verbal and tonal.

If you're high in tonal memory, you can take in information without taking notes. My sister is high in tonal memory. She used to knit in her college physics classes! She said the knitting helped her focus and listen better than note taking did!

Think about your fundraising appeals. Letters and brochures are great for people high in verbal memory. They read them and remember what they've read. But what about your donors high in tonal memory? Your well-crafted letters just don't work for them. Perhaps coming to an in-person event with speakers would be a better fit. Or maybe a monthly audio recording (CD or podcast) from your CEO would be appropriate.

We've only looked at a few of the more than 15 talents the Highlands identifies. By now you may be asking yourself, "This was supposed to make it easier for me to ask for money?!" I believe it will. Although we tend to act otherwise, we're all quite different. As fundraisers we need to pay attention to these differences. With the R.E.A.L. process, you've got the tools you need already to be an effective fundraiser, even without the content in this chapter. Knowing about D.I.S.C. and natural abilities will help you become incredibly effective, both in asking for money and in growing long-term relationships with people that love your organization!

8
Eight

Summary & Resources

Congratulations! Whether you're a committed volunteer or a paid staff member, you're much more equipped to go out and fund your favorite cause.

You've learned detailed ways to go about the "Get R.E.A.L." process: Research, Engage, Ask, and Love. You've explored the seven biggest mistakes we make when trying to raise money. You've learned how putting yourself in the donor's shoes can make your fundraising exponentially more successful. And you've been introduced to a couple of great tools to help you relate with other people more effectively and ask them to support your nonprofit in an approach that's tailored to them.

That's it. You're finished the book. But you're only just beginning your journey.

One of my favorite quotes from Glenn Bland's classic book Success, the Glenn Bland Method is:

"Shoot for the moon and if you miss, you can hit the eagle. Shoot for the eagle and miss, you'll hit the ground."

Setting high goals is an important thing. With a non-profit, you don't necessarily want to trumpet the highest goals. Nothing is more debilitating than announcing that you fell way short of your goals. But, we must get over our fear of what might happen and be tenacious in going after big gifts and not be afraid to jump into our thick skin suits. If we don't ask, we'll never know.

Use the R.E.A.L. steps. Better yet, try teaching them to someone you collaborate with. You'll internalize these four steps this week.

Please drop me a line if I can be of assistance. My email is marc@fundraisingcoach.com.

Resources

Research
Google.com

University of Vermont's Research Tools Page
http://www.uvm.edu/~prospect/index.html

Blackbaud Analytics http://www.blackbaud.com/

WeatlhEngine.com http://wealthengine.com/

P!N Electronic Screening http://www.prospectinfo.com/

Blackbaud Gift Range Calculator
http://www.blackbaud.com/resources/giftrange/giftcalc.aspx.

Engage
The Millionaire Next Door by Thomas Stanley and William Danko (1998)

Endless Referrals by Bob Burg

The Anatomy of Buzz by Emmanuel Rosen

Creating Customer Evangelists by Jackie Huba and Ben McConnell

Creating Donor Evangelists by Marc A. Pitman
(www.fundraisingcoach.com)

Ask
Asking by Jerry Panas

The Extreme Fundraising Blog by Marc A. Pitman
(www.fundraisingcoach.com)

Love
How to Win Friends and Influence People by Dale Carnegie

Growing Givers' Hearts by Thomas Jeavons and Rebekah Burch Basinger

Other
Life is Tremendous by Charlie "Tremendous" Jones

Success: The Glenn Bland Method by Glenn Bland

Highlands Ability Battery http://fundraisingcoach.com/highlands.htm

DISC http://www.personality-insights.com/

About the Author

Marc Pitman is a nationally-recognized thought leader and fundraising trainer. With over a decade of nonprofit experience and multiple campaigns, he's helped raise millions of dollars for all sorts of organizations: from schools to colleges, from hospitals to hospices, from community theaters to churches.

A noted expert quoted in media like Reuters and Successful Fundraising, Marc is a sought-after speaker at conferences and seminars, including teaching his popular "Creating Donor Evangelists" program. Through his seminars and one-on-one work, Marc helps his clients reconnect with the passion that got them into fundraising in the first place. When he's not helping others get passionate about raising money, he enjoys coffee, reading, and travel. Marc resides in Waterville, ME, with his incredible wife and three amazing kids.

For more great fundraising advice, go to Fundraisingcoach.com. There you'll find:
- free articles and book reviews
- tools to help you raise more money
- links to Marc's popular Extreme Fundraising Blog and free bi-weekly ezine
- and lots of helpful products in the Fundraising Coach Store.

More Resources

Now that you can confidently ask for money, learn how to "create donor evangelists"! Creating Donor Evangelists is created to teach you how you can make your organization stand out from the herd...without spending a ton of money.

Marc walks you through the four essential ingredients for creating passionate donors. He then leads you through a detailed, step-by-step recipe book of ideas and techniques that you can put into practice immediately!

Among the things you'll learn in this information rich program are:
• 4 practical ways to build buzz,
• 7 ways to build to create community within your donor base
• how the original Napster can help your nonprofit, and
• what food courts around that country know that may revolutionize your fundraising efforts
People say they love that Creating Donor Evangelists is:
• high quality,
• incredibly affordable, and
• incredibly easy to get up to speed in a very short period of time.

Creating Donor Evangelists is available as a booklet, an audio program, and on-demand multimedia seminars. All formats are available at: http://fundraisingcoach.com/cde.htm

Other Works by the Author

• The $100,000 Guide to E-mail Solicitation

• The MagnetGoals Goal Setting Workbook

• Creating Donor Evangelists: Moving Donors from Mere Check Writers to Raving Fans